Philosophy in the Present

Philosophy
in the Present

ALAIN BADIOU and SLAVOJ ŽIŽEK

Edited by Peter Engelmann

Translated by
PETER THOMAS and ALBERTO TOSCANO

polity

First published in German as *Philosophie und Aktualität. Ein Streitgespräch*
© Passagen Verlag, 2005

This English edition © Polity Press, 2009

Reprinted 2009, 2010 (three times)

Polity Press
65 Bridge Street
Cambridge CB2 1UR, UK

Polity Press
350 Main Street
Malden, MA 02148, USA

ISBN-13: 978-0-7456-4096-9 (hardback)
ISBN-13: 978-0-7456-4097-6 (paperback)

A catalogue record for this book is available from the British Library.

Designed and typeset in 12/17pt ITC Garamond Light
by Peter Ducker MISTD

Printed and bound in Great Britain
by the MPG Books Group

The publisher has used its best endeavours to ensure that the URLs for external websites referred to in this book are correct and active at the time of going to press. However, the publisher has no responsibility for the websites and can make no guarantee that a site will remain live or that the content is or will remain appropriate.

For further information on Polity, visit our website: www.politybooks.com

Contents

Editor's Preface   vii

ALAIN BADIOU
Thinking the Event   1

SLAVOJ ŽIŽEK
'Philosophy is not a Dialogue'   49

Discussion   73

Editor's Preface

The former French President François Mitterrand was known for inviting philosophers to the Élysée during his period in office in order to discuss political and social questions. He thus positioned himself in a long tradition in which enlightened power sought to come closer to the philosophers and to draw legitimacy from this proximity. We do not know whether or not these meetings influenced Mitterrand's political decisions, but at least he has remained in our memory as an intellectual president.

Whether their advice is earnestly sought or they are only used as decoration or intellectual cover, in reality the invited intellectuals usually don't come out of such performances particularly well. Nevertheless, being invited to the tables of power seems to exercise a great attraction for them.

The times when what philosophers like Simone de Beauvoir or Jean-Paul Sartre, Michel Foucault or Jean-François Lyotard had to say about contemporary events, or the suggestions they would make for the improvement of things, were regarded as important, belong to the past. Today, even the impersonators of philosophers who displaced philosophers in the 1970s have themselves been replaced by entertainers and models, by footballers and boxers.

We might therefore be tempted to speak of a golden age when the opinion of philosophers still seemed to count; but were they really better times?

It was not after all very long ago that we talked about what the role of the philosopher Karl Marx had been in the totalitarian regime of Russia, and later the countries of the Soviet bloc. Wasn't the mass murderer Pol Pot an intellectual educated in Paris? How many people were humiliated, expelled and murdered during the Chinese Cultural Revolution?

The question that governs this book, whether the philosopher should take part in contemporary events and comment on them, is the question regarding the role of intellectuals in our society, treated in a philosophically specific fashion. It no longer suffices to answer that the philosophers should not only interpret the world, but rather change it.

The answer to this question today must take into account two extremes. On the one hand, the participation of intellectuals in the crimes of the twentieth century weighs heavily on the self-understanding of this social group, at least insofar as it maintains a practical memory of history. On the other hand, we could ask ourselves if we really get a good deal if we let models, presenters, sportspeople and similar groups occupy the position of the intellectual in our contemporary media society.

The answers of the Parisian philosopher Alain Badiou and the Slovenian philosopher and psychoanalyst Slavoj Žižek during their discussion of this theme in Vienna 2004 turned out to be more modest and more sceptical than one might perhaps expect from philosophers. Instead of taking refuge in an old glory that has long since become historically obsolete, they try instead to recall the specific quality of philosophical thought and derive their answers from that.

Alain Badiou and Slavoj Žižek have known and esteemed one another for a long time. Slavoj Žižek was continually proposing Alain Badiou for the Passagen publishing programme. Badiou, for his part, has been helping to translate Žižek's work into French. Both know what the other will say and how he will argue, at least in broad outlines. They are not in agreement about important philosophical concepts and notions, as they affirm once again in this discussion. That is the case regarding their concepts of the event and the Real, but also for their understanding of the role of the imaginary or of politics. On the other hand, they agree that philosophical engagement must result out of the specificity of philosophical thought and should also establish its limits in this sense.

We owe the idea of this book to the initiative of François Laquièze, the former director of the French Cultural Institute in Vienna, who invited

Alain Badiou and Slavoj Žižek to Vienna for a public discussion. His partner in this initiative was Vincenc Rajšp, director of the Slovenian Scientific Institute in Vienna. The only specification was the theme; everything else was open to discussion, which was moderated by the Viennese journalist Claus Philipp.

During his time in Vienna, François Laquièze provided much stimulus to the exchange between French and German-language culture, and imparted a new vitality to the Institut Français of Vienna that is still observable in the city today. Above all, he was not afraid to complement the usual programme of cultural institutes with substantial contributions of contemporary thought and philosophy. We are in his debt.

We have avoided polishing the texts for publication. We consciously wanted to maintain the spontaneous character and not to distort the spoken word into a systematically grounded and articulated thought-structure. The book should, rather, stimulate contradiction, thought and further reading.

Perhaps Žižek is right that philosophy is not a dialogue. Philosophical discussion is nevertheless always stimulating, as the presentation and now this book demonstrate.

PETER ENGELMANN

Thinking the Event

ALAIN BADIOU

Tonight, we are asking ourselves: to what extent does philosophy intervene in the present, in historical and political questions? And in the end, what is the nature of this intervention? Why would the philosopher be called to intervene in questions regarding the present? We – Slavoj Žižek and I – are going to introduce this problem, and then discuss it. We are in agreement on many things, so we can't promise you a bloody battle. But we'll see what we can do.

There is a first, false idea that needs to be set aside, which is that the philosopher can speak about everything. This idea is exemplified by the TV philosopher: he talks about society's problems, the problems of the present, and so on. Why is this idea false? Because the philosopher constructs his own problems, he is an inventor of problems,

1

which is to say he is not someone who can be asked on television, night after night, what he thinks about what's going on. A genuine philosopher is someone who decides on his own account what the important problems are, someone who proposes new problems for everyone. Philosophy is first and foremost this: the invention of new problems.

It follows that the philosopher intervenes when in the situation – whether historical, political, artistic, amorous, scientific … – there are things that appear to him as signs, signs that it is necessary to invent a new problem. That's the point, the philosopher intervenes when he finds, in the present, the signs that point to the need for a new problem, a new invention. The question then becomes: on what conditions does the philosopher find, in the situation, the signs for a new problem, for a new thought? It is with regard to this point, and in order to lay out the grounds for our discussion, that I want to introduce the expression 'philosophical situation'. All sorts of things happen in the world, but not all of them are situations for philosophy, philosophical situations. So I would like us to ask the following question: what is a situation that is really a situation for philosophy, a situation for philosophical thought? I am going to offer you three examples, three examples of philosophical situations, in order to give you some grasp of what I am referring to.

The first example is already, if I can put it like this, philosophically formatted. It can be found in Plato's dialogue, *Gorgias*. This dialogue presents the extremely brutal encounter between Socrates and Callicles. This encounter creates a philosophical situation, which, moreover, is set out in an entirely theatrical fashion. Why? Because the thought of Socrates and that of Callicles share no common measure, they are totally foreign to one another. The discussion between Callicles and Socrates is written by Plato so as to make us understand what it means for there to be two different kinds of thought which, like the diagonal and the side of a square, remain incommensurable. This discussion amounts to a relation

3

between two terms devoid of any relation. Callicles argues that might is right, that the happy man is a tyrant – one who prevails over others through cunning and violence. Socrates on the contrary maintains that the true man, who is the same as the happy man, is the Just, in the philosophical sense of the term. Between justice as violence and justice as thought there is no simple opposition, of the kind that could be dealt with by means of arguments covered by a common norm. There is a lack of any real relation. Therefore the discussion is not a discussion; it is a confrontation. And what becomes clear to any reader of the text is not that one interlocutor will convince the other, but that there will be a victor and a vanquished. This is after all what explains why Socrates' methods in this dialogue are hardly fairer than those of Callicles. Wanting the ends means wanting the means, and it is a matter of winning, especially of winning in the eyes of the young men who witness the scene.

In the end, Callicles is defeated. He doesn't acknowledge defeat, but shuts up and remains in his corner. Note that he is the vanquished in a dialogue staged by Plato. This is probably one of the rare occurrences when someone like Callicles is the vanquished. Such are the joys of the theatre.

Faced with this situation, what is philosophy? The sole task of philosophy is to show that we must choose. We must choose between these two types of thought. We must decide whether we want to be on the side of Socrates or on the side of Callicles. In this example, philosophy confronts thinking as choice, thinking as decision. Its proper task is to elucidate choice. So that we can say the following: a philosophical situation consists in the moment when a choice is elucidated. A choice of existence or a choice of thought.

Second example: the death of the mathematician Archimedes. Archimedes is one of the greatest minds ever known to humanity. To this day, we are taken aback by his mathematical texts. He had already reflected on the infinite, and had practically invented infinitesimal calculus twenty centuries before Newton. He was an exceptional genius.

Archimedes was a Greek from Sicily. When Sicily was invaded and occupied by the Romans, he took part in the resistance, inventing new war machines – but the Romans eventually prevailed.

At the beginning of the Roman occupation, Archimedes resumed his activities. He was in the habit of drawing geometric figures on the sand. One day, as he sits thinking at the sea's edge, reflecting on the complicated figures he'd drawn on the shore, a Roman soldier arrives, a sort of courier, telling him that the Roman General Marcellus wishes to see him. The Romans were very curious about Greek scientists, a little like the CEO of a multinational cosmetics corporation might be curious about a philosopher of renown. So, General Marcellus wants to see Archimedes. Between us, I don't think we can imagine that General Marcellus was well up on mathematics. Simply, and this curiosity is a credit to him, he wanted to see what an insurgent of Archimedes' calibre was like. Whence the courier sent to the shore. But Archimedes doesn't budge. The soldier repeats: 'General Marcellus wishes to see you.' Archimedes still doesn't reply. The Roman soldier, who probably didn't have any great interest in mathematics either, doesn't understand how someone can ignore an order from General Marcellus. 'Archimedes! The General wishes to see you!' Archimedes barely looks up, and says to the soldier: 'Let me finish my demonstration.' And the soldier retorts: 'But Marcellus wants to see you! What do I care about your demonstration!' Without answering, Archimedes resumes his calculations. After a certain time, the soldier, by now absolutely furious, draws his sword and strikes him. Archimedes falls dead. His body effaces the geometrical figure in the sand.

Why is this a philosophical situation? Because it shows that between the right of the state and creative thought, especially the pure ontological thought embodied in mathematics, there is no common measure, no real discussion. In the end, power is violence, while the only constraints creative thought recognizes are its own immanent rules. When it comes to the law of his thought, Archimedes remains outside of the action of power. The temporality proper to the demonstration cannot integrate the urgent summons of military victors. That is why violence is eventually wrought, testifying that there is no common measure and no common chronology between the power of one side and the truths of the other. Truths as creation.

Let's recall in passing that during the US army's occupation of the suburbs of Vienna, at the end of the Second World War, a GI killed, obviously without recognizing who he was, the greatest musical genius of the time, the composer Anton Webern.

An accident. An accidental philosophical situation.

We can say that between power and truths there is a distance: the distance between Marcellus and Archimedes. A distance which the courier – no doubt an obtuse but disciplined soldier – does not manage to cross. Philosophy's mission is here to shed light on this distance. It must reflect upon and think a distance without measure, or a distance whose measure philosophy itself must invent.

First definition of the philosophical situation:

clarify the choice, the decision. Second definition of the philosophical situation: clarify the distance between power and truths.

My third example is a film. It is an astonishing film by the Japanese director Mizoguchi, entitled *The Crucified Lovers*. Without a doubt, it is one of the most beautiful films ever made about love. The plot can be easily summarized. The film is set in Japan's classical era, the visual qualities of which, especially when it comes to black and white, appear inexhaustible. A young woman is married to the owner of a small workshop, an honest man of comfortable means, but whom she neither loves nor desires. Enter a young man, one of her husband's employees, with whom she falls in love. But in this classical period, whose women Mizoguchi celebrated both in their endurance and their misfortune, adultery is punished by death: the culprits must be crucified. The two lovers end up fleeing to the countryside. The sequence which depicts their flight into the forest, into the world of paths, cabins, lakes and boats, is truly extraordinary. Love, prey to its own power over this hunted and harassed couple, is enveloped in a nature as opaque as it is poetic. All the while, the honest husband tries to protect the runaways. Husbands have the duty to denounce adulterers, they abhor the idea of turning into their accomplices. Nevertheless, the husband – and this is proof indeed that he genuinely loves his wife – tries to gain time. He pretends that his wife has left for the provinces, to see some relatives … A good, honest husband – really. A truly admirable character. But all the same, the lovers are denounced, captured, and taken to their torture.

There follow the film's final images, which constitute a new instance of the philosophical situation. The two lovers are tied back-to-back on a mule. The shot frames this image of the two bound lovers going to their atrocious death; both seem enraptured, but devoid of pathos: on their faces there is simply the hint of a smile, a kind of withdrawal into the smile. The word 'smile' here is only an approximation. Their faces reveal that

10

the man and the woman exist entirely in their love. But the film's thought, embodied in the infinitely nuanced black and white of the faces, has nothing to do with the romantic idea of the fusion of love and death. These 'crucified lovers' never desired to die. The shot says the very opposite: love is what resists death.

At a conference held at the Fémis, Deleuze, quoting Malraux, once said that art is what resists death. Well, in these magnificent shots, Mizoguchi's art not only resists death but leads us to think that love too resists death. This creates a complicity between love and art – one which in a sense we've always known about.

What I here name the 'smile' of the lovers, for lack of a better word, is a philosophical situation. Why? Because in it we once again encounter something incommensurable, a relation without relation. Between the event of love (the turning upside down of existence) and the ordinary rules of life (the laws of the city, the laws of marriage) there is no common measure. What will philosophy tell us then? It will tell us that 'we must think

11

the event'. We must think the exception. We must know what we have to say about what is not ordinary. We must think the transformation of life.

We can now sum up the tasks of philosophy with regard to situations.

First, to throw light on the fundamental choices of thought. 'In the last instance' (as Althusser would say) such choices are always between what is interested and what is disinterested.

Second, to throw light on the distance between thinking and power, between truths and the state. To measure this distance. To know whether or not it can be crossed.

Third, to throw light on the value of exception. The value of the event. The value of the break. And to do this against the continuity of life, against social conservatism.

These are the three great tasks of philosophy: to deal with choice, with distance and with the exception – at least if philosophy is to count for something in life, to be something other than an academic discipline.

At a deeper level, we can say that philosophy,

12

faced with circumstances, looks for the link between three types of situation – the link between choice, distance and the exception. I argue that a philosophical concept, in the sense that Deleuze speaks of it – which is to say as a creation – is always what knots together a problem of choice (or decision), a problem of distance (or gap), and a problem of the exception (or event).

The most profound philosophical concepts tell us something like this: 'If you want your life to have some meaning, you must accept the event, you must remain at a distance from power, and you must be firm in your decision.' This is the story that philosophy is always telling us, under many different guises: to be in the exception, in the sense of the event, to keep one's distance from power, and to accept the consequences of a decision, however remote and difficult they may prove.

Understood in this way, and only in this way, philosophy really is that which helps existence to be changed.

Ever since Rimbaud, everyone repeats that 'the true life is absent'. Philosophy is not worth an hour's effort if it is not based on the idea that the true life is present. With regard to circumstances, the true life is present in the choice, in distance and in the event.

Nevertheless, on the side of circumstances, we should not lose sight of the fact that we are forced to make a selection in order to attain the thought of the true life. This selection is founded, as we have said, on the criterion of incommensurability.

What unites our three examples is the fact that they are grounded on a relation between heterogeneous terms: Callicles and Socrates, the Roman soldier and Archimedes, the lovers and society.

The philosophical relationship to the situation stages the impossible relation, which takes the form of a story. We are told about the discussion between Callicles and Socrates, we are told about the murder of Archimedes, about the story of the crucified lovers. So, we hear the tale of a relation. But the story shows that this relation is not a relation, that it is the negation of relation. So that ultimately what

we are told about is a break: the break of the established natural and social bond. But of course, in
order to narrate a break, you first need to narrate
a relation. But in the end, the story is the story of
a break. Between Callicles and Socrates, one
must choose. It will be necessary to break
absolutely with one of the two. Similarly, if you side
with Archimedes, you can no longer side with
Marcellus. And if you follow the lovers in their jour-
ney to its very end, never again will you side with
the conjugal rule.

So we can say that philosophy, which is the
thought, not of what there is, but of what is not
what there is (not of contracts, but of contracts
broken), is exclusively interested in relations that
are not relations.

Plato once said that philosophy is an awakening. And he knew perfectly well that awakening
implies a difficult break with sleep. For Plato
already, and for all time, philosophy is the seizure
by thought of what breaks with the sleep of
thought.

So it is legitimate to think that each time there

is a paradoxical relation, that is, a relation which is not a relation, a situation of rupture, then philosophy can take place.

I insist on this point: it is not because there is 'something' that there is philosophy. Philosophy is not at all a reflection on anything whatsoever. There is philosophy, and there can be philosophy, because there are paradoxical relations, because there are breaks, decisions, distances, events.

We can throw some further light on this with examples which are neither legends, like the death of Archimedes, nor literary constructions, like the figure of Callicles, nor filmic poems, like the tale of the Japanese lovers. Let's take some good, simple contemporary examples. A negative one and a positive one.

My negative example is very simple. It concerns the reason why philosophers in general do not have anything interesting to say about electoral choices. Consider the usual situation of standard parliamentarianism. When you are confronted with electoral choices under standard parliamentarianism, you don't really possess any of the

criteria that justify and legitimate the intervention
of philosophy. I am not saying that one shouldn't
be interested in these situations. I am simply
saying that one cannot be interested in them in a
philosophical manner. When the philosopher
offers his views about these matters, he is an ordinary citizen, nothing more: he does not speak
from a position of genuine philosophical consis-
tency. So, why are things like this? Basically,
because in standard parliamentarianism, in its
usual functioning, the majority and the opposition
are commensurable. There is obviously a common
measure between the majority and the opposition,
which means you do not have a relation that is
not a relation, you do not have the paradoxical
relation. You have differences, naturally, but these
differences do not amount to a paradoxical relationship; on the contrary, they constitute a regular,
law-governed relationship. This is easily grasped:
since sooner or later (this is what is referred to as
'democratic alternation') the opposition will
replace the majority, or take its place, it is indeed
necessary for there to be a common measure

between the two. If you don't have a common measure, you will not be able to substitute the one with the other. So the terms are commensurable, and to the extent that they are commensurable you do not have the situation of radical exception. What's more, you do not have a truly radical choice: the decision is a decision between nuances, between small differences – as you know. Elections are generally decided by the small group of the hesitant, those who do not possess a stable, pre-formed opinion. People who have a genuine commitment constitute fixed blocs; then there is a small group of people in what is called the centre, who sometimes go one way, sometimes the other. And you can see why a decision taken by people whose principal characteristic is hesitation is a very particular decision; it is not a decision taken by decisive people, it is a decision of the undecided, or of those who have not decided and who will then decide for reasons of opportunity, or last-minute reasons. So the function of choice in its true breadth is absent. There is proximity, rather than distance. The election does not create a gap, it is the rule, it creates the realization of the rule. Finally, you do not have the hypothesis of a veritable event, you do not have the feeling of exception, because you are instead in the presence of the feeling of the institution, of the regular functioning of institutions. But there is obviously a fundamental tension between institution and exception. So the question of elections for the philosopher is a typical matter of opinion, which is to say that it doesn't have to do with the incommensurable, with radical choice, distance or exception. As a phenomenon of opinion, it does not constitute a sign for the creation of new problems.

My positive example concerns the necessity of an intervention faced with the American war against Iraq. In the case of the American war against Iraq, unlike in parliamentary elections, all the criteria are brought together. *First*, there is something incommensurable in a very simple sense: between American power, on the one hand, and the Iraqi state, on the other, there is no common measure. It's not like France and Germany during the war of 1914–18. In the war of 1914–18 there was a common measure between France and Germany, which is precisely why you could have a world war. Between the United States and Iraq there is no common measure of any kind. This absence of common measure is what lent all its significance to the whole business of 'weapons of mass destruction', because American and British propaganda about weapons of mass destruction sought to make people believe that there was a common measure. If Saddam Hussein effectively had atomic, chemical and biological weapons at his disposal, then you would have something that legitimated the intervention, in the sense of a common measure between American power and Iraq. You wouldn't be dealing with a war of aggression of the very strong against the very weak, but with legitimate defence against a measurable threat. The fact that there were no weapons of mass destruction makes patently clear what everyone already knew: that in this matter, there was no common measure. *Second*, you have the absolute necessity of a choice. This is the kind of situation in which it is not clear how one could be something other than either for or against this war. This obligation to choose is what gave the demonstrations and mobilizations against the war their breadth. *Third*, you have a distance from power: the popular demonstrations against the war create an important subjective gap with regard to the hegemonic power of the United States. Finally, you have, perhaps, the opening of a new situation marked, among other things, by the importance of these demonstrations, but also by new possibilities of common understanding and action between France and Germany.

Finally, with regard to what is happening, you must first of all ask: 'Is there a relation that is not a relation? Are there incommensurable elements?' If the answer is positive, you must draw the consequences: there is a choice, there is a distance, there is an exception. And on these bases, you can pass from the mere consideration of opinion to the philosophical situation. In these conditions, we can give meaning to philosophical commitment. This commitment creates its own conviction on the terrain of philosophy, making use of philosophical criteria.

I insist on the singularity of philosophical commitment. We must absolutely distinguish philosophy from politics. There are political commitments that are illuminated by philosophy, or even made necessary by philosophy, but philosophy and politics are distinct. Politics aims at the transformation of collective situations, while philosophy seeks to propose new problems for everyone. And this proposition concerning new philosophical problems constitutes an entirely different method, an entirely different form of judgement than the one which pertains to direct political militancy.

Of course, philosophy can work on the basis of political signs, it can constitute problems using political signs. But that does not mean that it can be confused with politics itself. This means that we can very easily imagine that, at a given moment, certain circumstances may be very important for politics, but not for philosophy, or vice versa. That is why philosophical commitment can sometimes seem very mysterious, even incomprehensible. Genuine philosophical commitment – the kind which is immersed in the incommensurable and summons the choice of thought, staging exceptions, creating distances and, especially, distancing from forms of power – is often a strange commitment.

There is a very interesting text by Plato on this point, a text that you can find at the end of Book IX of the *Republic*. As you know, in the *Republic*, Plato outlines a kind of political utopia. So that one could precisely think that in this book philosophy and politics are very close. At the end of Book IX, Socrates is discoursing with some youths, as always, and some among them say to him: 'This whole story's very nice, but it will never be realized anywhere.' The critique of utopia was already in place. So they say to him: 'Your Republic will never exist anywhere.' And Socrates replies: 'In any case, perhaps it will exist somewhere else than in our country.' In other words, he says that it will take place abroad, that there will be something foreign and strange about it. I think it is very important to understand this: genuine philosophical commitment, in situations, creates a foreignness. In a general sense, it is foreign. And when it is simply commonplace, when it does not possess this foreignness, when it is not immersed in this paradox, then it is a political commitment, an ideological commitment, the commitment of a citizen, but it is not necessarily a philosophical commitment. Philosophical commitment is marked by its internal foreignness.

This makes me think of a poem that I love very much, a poem by the French poet Saint-John Perse, a great epic poem called *Anabasis*. In this poem, at the end of section 5, you find the following lines, which I'd like to read to you: 'The Stranger, clothed in his new thoughts, acquires still more partisans in the ways of silence.' This is a definition of philosophical commitment. The philosopher is always a stranger, clothed in his new thoughts. This means that he proposes new thoughts and new problems. And he *acquires still more partisans in the ways of silence.* This means that he is capable of rallying a great number of

24

people to these new problems, because he has convinced them that these problems are universal. What matters is that those whom the philosopher addresses are convinced first of all through the silence of conviction and not through the rhetoric of discourse.

But as you can see, this figure of the stranger, who with his new thoughts makes companions for himself, often silent companions, rests entirely on the conviction that there are universal propositions, propositions addressed to the whole of humanity, without exception.

That is why I would like to add to this reflection about the commitment of the philosopher a necessary complement: that of a theory of universality. For, in the end, the philosopher commits himself with regard to a paradoxical situation in the name of universal principles. But what precisely does this universality consist in? I will respond in eight theses, eight theses on the universal. You will allow me to be a little more technical, a little more conceptual. It is something like a summary of my philosophy that I am attempting here before you. One cannot hope for the summary of a philosophy to be as simple as a sports summary. Even if philosophy, as Kant said, is a combat, which is to say a sport.

Here then, bit by bit, is my definition of the universal.

Thesis 1 Thought is the proper medium of the universal

By 'thought', I mean the subject insofar as it is constituted through a process that cuts through the totality of established knowledge. Or, as Lacan puts it, the subject insofar as it makes a hole in knowledge.

Remarks:

(a) That thought is the proper medium of the universal means that nothing exists as universal which takes the form of the object or of objective regularity. The universal is essentially 'anobjective'. It can be experienced only through the production (or reproduction) of a trajectory of

26

thought, and this trajectory constitutes (or reconstitutes) a subjective disposition.

Here are two typical examples: the universality of a mathematical proposition can only be experienced by inventing or effectively reproducing its proof; the situated universality of a political statement can only be experienced through the militant practice that effectuates it.

(b) That thought, as subject-thought, is constituted through a process means that the universal is in no way the result of a transcendental constitution, which would presuppose a constituting subject. On the contrary, the opening up of the possibility of a universal is the precondition for there being a subject-thought at the local level. The subject is invariably summoned as thought at a specific point of that procedure through which the universal is constituted. The universal is both what determines its own points as subject-thoughts and the virtual recollection of those points. Thus the central dialectic at work in the universal is that of the local as subject and of the global as infinite procedure. This dialectic is thought itself.

27

Consequently, the universality of the proposition 'the series of prime numbers is infinite' resides in the way it enjoins us to repeat (or rediscover) in thought a unique proof for it, but also in the global procedure that, from the Greeks to the present day, mobilizes number theory, along with its underlying axiomatic. To put it another way, the universality of the practical statement 'a country's illegal immigrant workers must have their rights recognized by that country' resides in all sorts of militant effectuations through which political subjectivity is actively constituted, but also in the global process of a politics, in terms of what it prescribes concerning the state and its decisions, rules and laws.

(c) That the process of the universal or truth – they are one and the same thing – is transversal relative to all available instances of knowledge means that the universal is always an incalculable emergence, rather than a describable structure. By the same token, I will say that a truth is intransitive to knowledge, and even that it is essentially unknown. That is another way of explaining what I mean when I characterize truth as unconscious.

I will call *particular* whatever can be discerned in knowledge by means of descriptive predicates. But I will call *singular* that which, although identifiable as a procedure at work in a situation, is nevertheless subtracted from every predicative description. Accordingly, the cultural traits of this or that population are particular. But that which, traversing these traits and deactivating every registered description, universally summons a thought-subject, is singular. Whence Thesis 2:

Thesis 2   Every universal is singular, or is a singularity

There is no possible universal sublation of particularity as such. It is commonly claimed nowadays that the only genuinely universal prescription consists in respecting particularities. In my opinion, this thesis is inconsistent. This is demonstrated by the fact that any attempt to put it into practice invariably runs up against particularities which the advocates of formal universality find intolerable. The truth is that in order to maintain that respect for particularity is a universal value, it is necessary to have first distinguished between good particularities and bad ones. In other words, it is necessary to have established a hierarchy in the list of descriptive predicates. It will be claimed, for example, that a cultural or religious particularity is bad if it does not include within itself respect for other particularities. But this is obviously to stipulate that the formal universal already be included in the particularity. Ultimately, the universality of respect for particularities is only the universality of universality. This definition is fatally tautological. It is the necessary counterpart of a protocol – usually a violent one – that wants to eradicate genuinely particular particularities (i.e. immanent particularities) because it freezes the predicates of the latter into self-sufficient identitarian combinations.

Thus it is necessary to maintain that every universal presents itself not as a regularization of the particular or of differences, but as a singularity that is subtracted from identitarian predicates; although obviously it proceeds via those predicates. The subtraction of particularities must be opposed to their supposition. But if a singularity can lay claim to the universal by subtraction, it is because the play of identitarian predicates, or the logic of those forms of knowledge that describe particularity, precludes any possibility of foreseeing or conceiving it.

Consequently, a universal singularity is not of the order of being, but of the order of an upsurge. Whence Thesis 3:

Thesis 3 Every universal originates in an event, and the event is intransitive to the particularity of the situation

The correlation between universal and event is fundamental. Basically, it is clear that the question of political universalism depends entirely on the regime of fidelity or infidelity maintained, not to this or that doctrine, but to the French Revolution, or the Paris Commune, or October 1917, or the struggles for national liberation, or May 1968. Contrariwise, the negation of political universalism,

31

the negation of the very theme of emancipation, requires more than mere reactionary propaganda. It requires what could be called an *evental revisionism*. Take, for example, Furet's attempt to show that the French Revolution was entirely futile; or the innumerable attempts to reduce May 1968 to a student stampede towards sexual liberation. Evental revisionism targets the connection between universality and singularity. To quote Mallarmé, nothing took place but the place, predicative descriptions are sufficient, and whatever is universally valuable is strictly objective. Ultimately, this amounts to the claim that whatever is universally valuable resides in the mechanisms and power of capital, along with its statist guarantees.

In that case, the fate of the human animal is sealed by the relation between predicative particularities and legislative generalities – an animalistic fate.

For an event to initiate a singular procedure of universalization, and to constitute its subject through that procedure, is contrary to the positivist coupling of particularity and generality.

In this regard, the case of sexual difference is significant. The predicative particularities identifying the positions 'man' and 'woman' within a given society can be conceived in an abstract fashion. A general principle can be posited whereby the rights, status, characteristics and hierarchies associated with these positions should be subject to egalitarian regulation by the law. That's all well and good, but it does not provide a ground for any sort of universality as far as the predicative distribution of gender roles is concerned. For this to be the case, there has to be the suddenly emerging singularity of an encounter or declaration: one that crystallizes a subject whose manifestation is precisely its subtractive experience of sexual difference. Such a subject comes about through an amorous encounter in which there occurs a disjunctive synthesis of sexuated positions. Thus the amorous scene is the only genuine scene in which a universal singularity pertaining to the Two of the sexes – and ultimately pertaining to difference as such – is proclaimed. That is where an undivided subjective experience of absolute difference takes place. It is well known that, where the interplay between the sexes is concerned, people are invariably fascinated by love stories; and this fascination is directly proportional to the various specific obstacles through which social formations try to thwart love. In this instance, it is perfectly clear that the attraction exerted by the universal lies precisely in the fact that it subtracts itself (or tries to subtract itself) as an asocial singularity from the predicates of knowledge.

Thus, it is necessary to maintain that the universal emerges as a singularity and that all we have to begin with is a precarious supplement whose sole strength lies in there being no available predicate capable of subjecting it to knowledge.

The question then is: What material instance, what unclassifiable effect of presence, provides the basis for the subjectivating procedure whose main characteristic is the universal?

Thesis 4 A universal initially presents itself as a decision about an undecidable

This point requires careful elucidation.

I call 'encyclopaedia' the general system of predicative knowledge internal to a situation: i.e. what everyone knows about politics, sexual difference, culture, art, technology, etc. There are certain things, statements, configurations or discursive fragments whose valence is not decidable in terms of the encyclopaedia. Their valence is uncertain, floating, anonymous: they exist at the margins of the encyclopaedia. They comprise everything whose status remains constitutively uncertain; everything that elicits a 'maybe, maybe not'; everything whose status can be endlessly debated according to the rule of non-decision, which is itself encyclopaedic; everything about which knowledge enjoins us not to decide. Nowadays, for instance, knowledge enjoins us not to decide about God: it is quite acceptable to maintain that perhaps 'something' exists, or perhaps it does not. We live in a society in which no valence can be ascribed to God's existence; one that lays claim to a vague spirituality. Similarly, knowledge enjoins us not to decide about the possible existence of 'another politics': it is talked about, but nothing comes of it. Another example: Are those workers who do not have proper papers but who are working here, in France, part of this country? Do they belong here? 'Probably, since they live and work here.' Or: 'No, since they don't have the necessary papers to show that they are French, or living here legally'. The term 'illegal immigrant' [*clandestin*] designates the uncertainty of valence, or the non-valence of valence: it designates people who are living here, but don't really belong here, and hence people who can be thrown out of the country, people who can be exposed to the non-valence of the valence of their presence here as workers.

Basically, an event is what decides about a zone of encyclopaedic indiscernibility. More precisely, there is an implicative function of the type: $E \rightarrow d(\varepsilon)$, which reads as: every real subjectivation brought about by an event, which disappears in its appearance, implies that ε, which is undecidable within the situation, has been decided. This was the case, for example, when illegal immigrant workers occupied the church of St Bernard in Paris: they publicly declared the existence and valence of what had been without valence, thereby deciding that those who are here belong here and enjoining people to drop the expression 'illegal immigrant' [*clandestin*].

I will call ε the evental statement. By virtue of the logical rule of *detachment*, we see that the abolition of the event, whose entire being consists in disappearing, leaves behind the evental statement ε, which is implied by the event, as something that is:

– a real of the situation (since it was already there);
– but something whose valence undergoes radical change, since it was undecidable but has been decided. It is something that had no valence but now does.

Consequently, I will say that the inaugural

materiality for any universal singularity is the evental statement. It fixes the present for the subject-thought out of which the universal is woven.

Such is the case in an amorous encounter, whose subjective present is fixed in one form or another by the statement 'I love you', even as the circumstance of the encounter is erased. Thus, an undecidable disjunctive synthesis is decided and the inauguration of its subject is tied to the consequences of the evental statement.

Note that every evental statement has a declarative structure, regardless of whether the statement takes the form of a proposition, a work, a configuration or an axiom. The evental statement is implied by the event's appearing-disappearing and declares that an undecidable has been decided or that what was without valence now has a valence. The constituted subject follows in the wake of this declaration, which opens up a possible space for the universal.

Accordingly, all that is required in order for the universal to unfold is to draw all the consequences, within the situation, of the evental statement.

Thesis 5   The universal has an implicative form

A common objection to the idea of universality is
that everything that exists or is represented relates
back to particular conditions and interpretations
governed by disparate forces or interests. Thus, for
instance, some maintain it is impossible to attain
a universal grasp of difference because of the abyss
between the ways the latter is grasped, depending
on whether one occupies the position of 'man' or
the position of 'woman'. Still others insist that there
is no common denominator underlying what various cultural groups choose to call 'artistic activity';
or that not even a mathematical proposition is intrin-
sically universal, since its validity is entirely
dependent upon the axioms that support it.

What this hermeneutic perspectivalism over-
looks is that every universal singularity is pre-
sented as the network of consequences entailed
by an evental decision. What is universal always
takes the form $\varepsilon \rightarrow \pi$, where ε is the evental statement and π is a consequence, or a fidelity. It
goes without saying that if someone refuses the

decision about ε, or insists, in reactive fashion, on reducing ε to its undecidable status, or maintains that what has taken on a valence should remain without valence, then the implicative form in no way enjoins them to accept the validity of the consequence, π. Nevertheless, even they will have to admit the universality of the form of implication as such. In other words, even they will have to admit that if the event is subjectivated on the basis of its statement, whatever consequences come to be invented as a result will be necessary.

On this point, Plato's apologia in the *Meno* remains irrefutable. If a slave knows nothing about the evental foundation of geometry, he remains incapable of validating the construction of the square of the surface that doubles a given square. But if one provides him with the basic data and he agrees to subjectivate it, he will also subjectivate the construction under consideration. Thus, the implication that inscribes this construction in the present inaugurated by geometry's Greek emergence is universally valid.

Someone might object: 'You're making things

too easy for yourself by invoking the authority of mathematical inference.' But they would be wrong. Every universalizing procedure is implicative. It verifies the consequences that follow from the evental statement to which the vanished event is indexed. If the protocol of subjectivation is initiated under the aegis of this statement, it becomes capable of inventing and establishing a set of universally recognizable consequences.

The reactive denial that the event took place, as expressed in the maxim 'nothing took place but the place', is probably the only way of undermining a universal singularity. It refuses to recognize its consequences and cancels whatever present is proper to the evental procedure.

Yet even this refusal cannot cancel the universality of implication as such. Take the French Revolution: if, from 1792 onwards, this constitutes a radical event, as indicated by the immanent declaration which states that revolution as such is now a political category, then it is true that the citizen can only be constituted in accordance with the dialectic of virtue and terror. This implication

is both undeniable and universally transmissible –
in the writings of Saint-Just, for instance. But obviously, if one thinks there was no revolution, then
virtue as a subjective disposition does not exist
either and all that remains is the terror as an out-
burst of insanity requiring moral condemnation.
Yet even if politics disappears, the universality of
the implication that puts it into effect remains.

There is no need to invoke a conflict of interpretations here. This is the nub of my sixth thesis:

Thesis 6 The universal is univocal

Insofar as subjectivation occurs through the consequences of the event, there is a univocal logic
proper to the fidelity that constitutes a universal
singularity.

Here we have to go back to the evental statement. Recall that the statement circulates within a
situation as something undecidable. There is
agreement both about its existence and its unde-
cidability. From an ontological point of view, it is
one of the multiplicities of which the situation is

composed. From a logical point of view, its valence is intermediary or undecided. What occurs through the event does not have to do with the being that is at stake in the event, nor with the meaning of the evental statement. It pertains exclusively to the fact that, whereas previously the evental statement had been undecidable, henceforth it will have been decided, or decided as true. Whereas previously the evental statement had been devoid of significance, it now possesses an exceptional valence. This is what happened with the illegal immigrant workers who demonstrated their existence at the St Bernard church.

In other words, what affects the statement, insofar as the latter is bound up in an implicative manner with the evental disappearance, is of the order of the *act*, rather than of being or meaning. It is precisely the register of the act that is univocal. It just so happened that the statement was decided, and this decision remains subtracted from all interpretation. It relates to the yes or the no, not to the equivocal plurality of meaning.

What we are talking about here is a logical act,

or even, as one might say echoing Rimbaud, a logical revolt. The event decides in favour of the truth or eminent valence of that which the previous logic had confined to the realm of the undecidable or of non-valence. But for this to be possible, the univocal act that modifies the valence of one of the components of the situation must gradually begin to transform the logic of the situation in its entirety. Although the being-multiple of the situation remains unaltered, the logic of its appearance – the system that evaluates and connects all the multiplicities belonging to the situation – can undergo a profound transformation. It is the trajectory of this mutation that composes the encyclopaedia's universalizing diagonal.

The thesis of the equivocity of the universal refers the universal singularity back to those generalities whose law holds sway over particularities. It fails to grasp the logical act that universally and univocally inaugurates a transformation in the entire structure of appearance.

For every universal singularity can be defined as follows: It is the act to which a subject-thought becomes bound in such a way as to render that act capable of initiating a procedure which effects a radical modification of the logic of the situation, and hence of what appears insofar as it appears.

Obviously, this modification can never be fully accomplished. For the initial univocal act, which is always localized, inaugurates a fidelity, i.e. an invention of consequences, which will prove to be as infinite as the situation itself. Whence Thesis 7:

Thesis 7 Every universal singularity remains incompletable or open

The only commentary required by this thesis concerns the manner in which the subject, the localization of a universal singularity, is bound up with the infinite, the ontological law of being-multiple. On this particular issue, it is possible to show that there is an essential complicity between the philosophies of finitude, on the one hand, and relativism, or the negation of the universal and the discrediting of the notion of truth, on the other. Let me put it in terms of a single maxim: The latent violence, the presumptuous arrogance inherent in the currently prevalent conception of human rights derives from the fact that these are actually the rights of finitude and ultimately – as the insistent theme of democratic euthanasia indicates – the rights of death. By way of contrast, the evental conception of universal singularities, as Jean-François Lyotard remarked in *The Differend*, requires that human rights be thought of as the rights of the infinite. One can also say: the rights of infinite affirmation. I would say even more exactly: the rights of the generic.

Thesis 8 Universality is nothing other than the faithful construction of an infinite generic multiple

What do I mean by generic multiplicity? Quite simply, a subset of the situation that is not determined by any of the predicates of encyclopaedic knowledge; that is to say, a multiple such that to belong to it, to be one of its elements, cannot be the result of having an identity, of possessing any particular property. If the universal is for everyone, this is in the precise sense that to be inscribed within it is not a matter of possessing any particular determination. This is the case with political gatherings, whose universality follows from their indifference to social, national, sexual or generational origin; with the amorous couple, which is universal because it produces an undivided truth about the difference between sexed positions; with scientific theory, which is universal to the extent that it removes every trace of its provenance in its elaboration; or with artistic configurations, whose subjects are works, and in which, as Mallarmé remarked, the particularity of the author has been abolished, so much so that in exemplary inaugural configurations, such as the *Iliad* and the *Odyssey*, the proper name that underlies them – Homer – ultimately refers back to nothing but the void of any and every subject.

Thus the universal arises according to the chance of an aleatory supplement. It leaves behind it a simple detached statement as a trace of the disappearance of the event that founds it. It initiates its procedure in the univocal act through which the valence of what was devoid of valence comes to be decided. It binds to this act a subject-thought who will invent consequences for it. It faithfully constructs an infinite generic multiplicity, which, by its very opening, is what Thucydides declared his written history of the Peloponnesian war – unlike the latter's historical particularity – would be: *ktema es aiei*, 'a possession forever'.

There we are. If you combine the eight theses on the universal and the definition of paradoxical situations, you have the means with which to answer the question of the commitment of philosophers in the present.

'Philosophy is not a Dialogue'
SLAVOJ ŽIŽEK

There will hardly be a dialogue between us because we are to a large extent in agreement. Could that be, however – to begin with a provocation – a sign of real philosophy? I am of the same opinion as Badiou when he emphasizes, with Plato, that philosophy is axiomatic, and asks how the true philosophy could actually be known. You're sitting in a café and someone challenges you: 'Come on, let's discuss that in depth!' The philosopher will immediately say, 'I'm sorry, I must leave', and will make sure he disappears as quickly as possible.

I have always considered Plato's late dialogues to be his philosophical dialogues in the true sense of the word. In them, one person speaks almost without interruption; the objections of the others – in the *Sophist* – for example, would hardly fill half a page. They say, for example, 'You are completely right', 'Quite clearly', 'It is so.' And why not? Philosophy is not a dialogue. Name me a single example of a successful philosophical dialogue that wasn't a dreadful misunderstanding. This is true also for the most prominent cases: Aristotle didn't understand Plato correctly; Hegel – who might have been pleased by the fact – of course didn't understand Kant. And Heidegger fundamentally didn't understand anyone at all. So, no dialogue. But let's go on.

I will approach the problem in the usual way. It's true: today, we philosophers are addressed, questioned and challenged; it is expected that we intervene, that we become engaged in the European public sphere and so forth. How should we react to these demands? Not in a very different way, I think – of course, not exactly the same way – from how a psychoanalyst responds to a patient: for the patient also demands something. Only rarely does he or she exhaust these demands. They are false demands; they allude to a real problem that they simultaneously conceal. Let's go back to the theme of incommensurability mentioned by Alain

Badiou. In his terrific essay about September 11, he takes up the Deleuzian concept of the 'disjunctive synthesis'. If one asks us philosophers something, in general something more is involved than providing public opinion with some orientation in a problematic situation. For example: today we are in a war against terror, and that confronts us with daunting problems: should we trade our freedom for security from terror? Should we carry liberal openness to extremes – even if this means cutting off our roots and losing our identity – or should we assert our identity more strongly? To point out that the alternatives we collectively face form a disjunctive synthesis, that is, that they are false alternatives, has to be the first gesture of the philosopher here: he must change the very concepts of the debate – which in my opinion represents precisely the negative of that which Badiou calls a 'radical choice'. In our case, concretely, it means that 'liberalism', 'war against terror' and so-called 'fundamentalist terrorism' are all disjunctive syntheses; they are not the radical choice. We must change the concepts of the debate. To give a further example:

in the summer of 2003, the great European philosophers, Derrida and Habermas, as well as some others, among whom even some Americans, honourably intervened in the public sphere and pleaded for a new Europe. Doesn't that speak volumes about their philosophical positions? This is always the case: political agreement among philosophers betrays something about their philosophy. Take Richard Rorty, with whom philosophically I don't agree at all, but who I regard as an intelligent liberal, not afraid of pointing out the obvious – a task that more discriminating but impotent liberals are always too dignified to carry out. He tells us what's going on when people like him, Derrida, Habermas and (from the cognitive field) Daniel Dennett engage in philosophical debate. A glance at their political positions reveals another picture: irrespective of their philosophical positions, they are all a little to the left of the democratic middle. On with democracy, perhaps even a little more, is Rorty's typical pragmatic conclusion. That shows that philosophy is inconsequential. Is that really the case? Let's consider the political agreement of Habermas and Derrida as a paradigmatic case: could that not be an indication of the fact that their philosophical positions are also not really incommensurable? That even their opposition is merely a disjunctive synthesis?

If you look at the structure of their thought more closely, this supposition is confirmed: fundamentally, both are concerned in the same way with the problem of communication, or more precisely with a communication that opens to the other, recognizes him and leaves him his otherness, instead of damaging it. We are dealing here, I believe, merely with two complementary versions, even if Habermas claims an undamaged communication with the other and his unique order, while Derrida emphasizes precisely the opposite: we should open ourselves to the radical contingency of the other. Badiou's great service, against these mutually complementary positions, as it appears to me, is to have changed the entire field with his ethics. Otherness is not the problem, but rather, the Same. For me, this should be the philosopher's first gesture, when he is pressured with demands. To change the concepts of the debate itself – now, for example, virtual reality is a fashionable theme; we live in a virtual universe: do we lose contact with authentic reality? Have we completely alienated ourselves? Here we meet again the disjunctive synthesis: we can think of postmodernists whose wonderful nomadic subjectivity could shift from one artificial reality to the next; or nostalgic conservatives and left-conservatives for whom that would be a shame and who say that we must turn back instead to authentic experience. We should do something different: namely, reject the concepts of the debate and claim, not that virtual reality is the problem, but rather, the reality of the virtual. How is that?

I mean: virtual reality – Badiou has written that somewhere – is a relatively banal idea. It doesn't give us anything to think. Virtual reality, that means: 'look how we can create with our technical toys an appearance that in the end we believe to be reality.' In my view, it is the reality of the virtual which is interesting for thought. The virtual is any particular thing, but nothing whole;

it is – if you want – the actual effect of the real. Here is the actual problem.

Let's go to the next theme that stimulates journalism: hedonism. We should also take up a position regarding hedonism. What is to be done when the old values fall away and humans lose their belief, cultivate egotism and dedicate their life only to the pursuit of pleasures? Once again, the field is divided into two camps: every fixed moral attitude includes an act of violence – Judith Butler represents this typical postmodern attitude in her last book, still only available in German, *Zur Kritik der ethischen Gewalt*[1] – we must thus be flexible and so on, which runs up against the theme of nomadic subjectivity once again; fixed values and connections are what the country needs – that is the answer from the other side. Of course, we should here once again tackle the problem directly and put the concepts of the

[1] Suhrkamp 2003. [Translator's note: this was the printed version of Butler's Adomo-Vorlesungen 2002 at the Institut für Sozialforschung at the Johann Wolfgang Goethe-Universität, Frankfurt am Main. A reworked version is now available in English in *Giving An Account of Oneself*, New York, Fordham University Press, 2005.]

debate in question, with a type of Brechtian *Ver-fremdung*; the thing itself will thus become strange to us: 'But wait a minute? What are we speaking about here?' About hedonism in a consumer society whose chief characteristic is a radical pro-hibition: enjoy immediately. It is always: 'Of course you should enjoy, but in order really to be able to enjoy, first you have to go jogging, go on a diet and you shouldn't be sexually harassing anybody.' At the end is total body discipline. But let's go back to the belief, to the cliché that today we have lost belief. This is nothing more than a pseudo-debate: today we believe more than ever – and this is the problem, as Robert Pfaller has shown. The concepts of the debate are therefore no longer the same. Unfortunately, however, the great majority of philosophers haven't stepped up to the challenges at this high level, and thus they burden us with false answers.

The worst are of course answers in the style of New Age monstrosities, which do not deserve the honour of being called philosophy. We can all think of some interesting examples here. Try comparing – if you are old enough, which I am and also some of you unfortunately are too – a typical social sciences and humanities bookshop of today with one from twenty-five years ago. Today, unfortunately, there is three times as much talk of wisdom, enlightenment and the New Age – and correspondingly less of philosophy. So much for the first false answer, which of course was already too much anyway. Two other false answers appear to me to be much more problematic. Which? I'd like to refer here once again to Badiou, who stresses that philosophy and politics should not be confused with each other. He claims in his text on the end of communism that the problem in relation to totalitarianism is that we still don't have an appropriate socio-political theory with which we can analyse these of course deplorable phenomena like Nazism and Stalinism in their own conceptuality as political projects. To give a philosophical fast food answer, passing itself off as a deep explanation, which in truth is only a substitute that allows us to dispense with thinking, would be the worst thing that a philosopher can do here – and unfortunately usually does. Perhaps you will be surprised here, but my high regard for Adorno doesn't stop me from saying that here lies the problem of the *Dialectic of Enlightenment*. Instead of concrete analysis, we are offered a prime example of philosophical (in the negative sense of the word) confusion, a type of politico-ontological short circuit: the pseudo-transcendental category of the 'project of the enlightenment' is supposed to explain immediately the totalitarian phenomena. A more recent version of this pseudo and false philosophical gesture, whose philosophy *prevents* us from thinking, is the postmodern short circuit of political totalitarianism with the philosophical concept of totality: here one evokes the ontological unveiling as immediate, almost transcendental explanation of concrete political phenomena. Postmodern philosophy offers the appearance of thought, in order to discredit before the fact any event – in the Badiouian sense of the rupturing new. That is also what is afoot during the last ten or fifteen years in regard to the Holocaust and other forms of unimaginable

radical evil: the prohibition to analyse these phenomena – we are only allowed to witness them,
any explanation would already be a betrayal of the
victims …

The foundation of this idea, I believe, is the idea
that we have to live with our imperfect world,
since any radical alternative sooner or later would
lead to the Gulag. We are warned against any radical change. Indeed, the whole discourse of
opening ourselves to the radical otherness is
merely this warning of the radical change! So that
is the postmodern philosophical ideology. Next to
this we find something else, equally interesting: a
type of neo-Kantianism. In France, it is represented by Alain Renault, as well as Luc Ferry, who
is even Minister for Education at the moment; in
Germany, its representative is Habermas, who –
whether he likes it or not – today, as is well
known, functions as a state philosopher; what is
often only implied was explicitly confirmed by
Aznar when he suggested two years ago the
appointment of Habermas as Spain's official state
philosopher. How can that be?

I have sought to solve this dilemma, as I believe, successfully. A certain neo-Kantianism fits the definition of state philosophy perfectly (I say that despite my love for Kant). What is the chief function of state philosophy in the contemporary dynamic capitalist society? It should endorse the development, indispensable for capitalism, of new sciences, of technology and business, while at the same time, however, it should obstruct their radical ethical and social consequences. This is precisely what Habermas has done, at least with his intervention in the biogenetic debate. He presents us with a typical neo-Kantian solution: in the sciences you can do whatever you want; remember, however, that we are dealing only with the narrow field of cognitive phenomena. The human as autonomously acting moral subject is something else, and this field must be defended from every threat. With that, however, all of these pseudo-problems emerge: how far are we allowed to go into biogenetics? Does biogenetics threaten our freedom and autonomy? In my opinion, these are false questions; at any rate, they are not real philosophical questions. The only real philosophical question is instead the following: is there something in the results of biogenetics that would force us to redefine what we understand by human nature, by the human way of being?

It is quite sad to see how Habermas tries to control the explosive results of biogenetics, to contain their philosophical consequences. His whole intervention betrays the fear that something could fundamentally change, that a new dimension of the 'human' could emerge and the old idea of human dignity and autonomy would not be safely conserved. His overreactions are here characteristic, for example, in the case of Sloterdijk's Elmauer talk on biogenetics and Heidegger: when Sloterdijk said that biogenetics forces us to formulate new rules of ethics, Habermas heard only the echo of National Socialist eugenics. This attitude towards scientific progress issues in a 'temptation of the temptation (to resist)': the temptation which we must resist is the pseudo-moralistic attitude that represents the discovery of science as temptation, which lets us 'go too far' – in the forbidden field (of biogenetic manipulation and so forth) – thus endangering the innermost core of our human being itself.

The recent moral 'crisis' provoked by biogenetics actually culminates in the need for a philosophy that we are completely justified in calling a 'state philosophy': a philosophy which, on the one hand, tacitly tolerates scientific and technical progress, while on the other hand, it tries to control its effects on our socio-symbolic order, that is, to prevent the existing theological-ethical world picture from changing. It is no wonder that those who go the furthest in this are neo-Kantians: Kant himself confronted the problem of how he could account for Newtonian science but at the same time guarantee that there would be a realm of moral responsibility lying outside of science. He limited the field of validity of knowledge in order to create room for belief and morality. Don't the contemporary state philosophers face the same task? Isn't their effort directed towards the question of how – by means of different versions of transcendental reflection – science can be limited to its fixed horizon of meaning and its consequences can be denounced as 'inadmissible' for the moral-religious field? Interestingly, Sloterdijk's proposal of a 'humanist' synthesis of new scientific truths and the old horizon of meaning, even if he is more refined and ironic-sceptical than the Habermasian 'state philosophy', only differs from it in the end by an unverifiable line of demarcation (or to be more precise: Sloterdijk's proposal oscillates between the Habermasian compromise and the New Age monstrosities).

While we are speaking about philosophy and politics: here, I believe, also lies the general explanation for the demise of the Frankfurt school. What is the outcome of the Frankfurt school? How can it be conceptualized? Its fundamental statement is the *Dialectic of Enlightenment*: the idea that the modern project of emancipation has a structural flaw; all of these terrible things, totalitarianism and the like, are not residues of the past, but its logical product. Let me once more approach this like a simpleton. I would then say: Stalinist communism had to be the prime example of this. For – to say it with extremely simplified and stupid concepts – fascism was a conservative reaction. There were people behind it who – again, to express it in an admittedly naïve way – intended to do something incredibly evil and actually did it (what a surprise!). The real trauma, however, is Stalinism. The communist project – I hope you agree with me – opened with a strong emancipatory potential – and went wrong. That is the trauma of the dialectic of enlightenment; but what do we find in critical theory? Nothing of this. There is Neumann's *Behemoth*, the worst type of journalistic sociology that can be imagined, based on the fashionable idea of a convergence, according to which Roosevelt's America of the New Deal, Nazi Germany and the Soviet Union tended towards the same organized society. There is Marcuse's *Soviet Marxism*: a very peculiar book, which never precisely explains its author's position. Then there are some attempts by Habermasians, like Andrew Arato, to play off the idea of civil society as place of existence against totalitarian communist dominance. But even here we don't have any theory that helps us to explain Stalinist communism. By the way, I believe that the theory of civil society is completely mistaken. At any rate, I should say that in the break-up of Yugoslavia just as in most other conflicts between the state and civil society, I was regularly on the side of the state. Civil society meant democratic opposition; it also meant, however, violent nationalism. The formula of Milosevic described precisely this highly explosive mixture of nationalist civil society and the party nomenclature. The dissidents demanded a dialogue between the party nomenclature and civil society, and Milosevic actually did this.

Let's take Habermas: does reading his books betray the fact that half of his homeland, Germany, was socialist? No. It is as if this matter of fact didn't exist. I believe that this is, with a fashionable concept, a type of symptomatic gap, an empty place.

I will now speak a little more briefly. I want to conclude with a remark about the possible role of philosophy in our society. There is a whole series of false philosophical positions: neo-Kantian state philosophy, postmodern neo-Sophism and so forth. The worst is the external moralization of philosophy, the logic of which is roughly the following: 'I am a philosopher, and as such I devise great metaphysical systems; I am also however a good human and am concerned about all the disaster in this world. We must struggle against this disaster ...' Derrida is weakest at that point when, in the middle of his book *Spectres of Marx*, he becomes entirely unphilosophical and lists the disasters in this world in ten points. Unbelievable! I didn't believe my eyes as I read that; but there they were, ten points; and they attested to an extreme lack of thought: unemployment and dropouts without money in our cities; drug cartels; the domination of the media monopolies and so forth. As if he wanted to give the impression of being not merely a great philosopher but also a warm-hearted person. Excuse me, but here I can think of only a relatively fatal comparison: at the end of works of popular literature there is usually a short description of the author – and in order to

valorize their curriculum a little, one adds something like: 'she currently lives in the South of
France, surrounded by many cats and dedicated
to painting …' That is more or less the level we're
dealing with. It almost prompts me therefore to
add something mischievous to my next books: 'In
his private life he tortures dogs and kills spiders',
simply in order to push this custom *ad absurdum.*
But I want to go on: if we philosophers are asked
for our opinion, often all one wants in truth is that
we introduce ourselves. Our knowledge is then a
type of vague reference that gives an authority to
our opinions. It is just as if one asked a great
author what he likes to eat, and he answers that
Italian cooking is better than Chinese cooking. We
should therefore only concern ourselves with
what is inherent to philosophy.

What is then the role of philosophy? Here we
confront a paradox: philosophy hardly ever, and
least of all in its creative periods, plays a normal
role in the sense that it is merely philosophy. Here
are a couple of unrelated facts: in the nineteenth
century, literature in some nations, like Hungary

and Poland, often played the role of philosophy; for example, the philosophical or ideological vision that lay at the foundations of the national movement was formulated to a large extent in literature. Even in the United States, for example, in ninety-nine out of one hundred cases, you won't find so-called *continental philosophy* in the philosophy faculties (and that is to be taken literally: out of 4,000 US colleges with a philosophical faculty, only fifteen to twenty of them have any real representation of continental philosophy). Instead, we find it in cultural studies, in English, in French and German departments. If you want to read Hegel and Badiou, you must paradoxically choose comparative literature with majors in French and German. If, on the other hand, you do research on the brains of rats and perform experiments on animals, you go to the philosophical faculties. But it is not uncommon that philosophy occupies the place of another subject: when, for example, communism fell apart, philosophy was the first place in which the resistance was formulated. It was more political than ever at this point in time. However, here you might like to object that great German philosophy was nothing but philosophy. Absolutely not! Already with Heine, not just with Marx, we know that philosophy was the German substitute for the revolution. That is the dilemma: you can't have both. It is false to claim that the French could have had philosophy if only they had been clever enough. Conversely, the non-appearance of the revolution was the condition for German philosophy. My idea is now the following: perhaps we have to break with the dream that there is a normal philosophy. Perhaps philosophy is abnormality par excellence. Thus I would read Badiou's theory. (We, Badiou and I, embrace each other, but in reality we hate each other. Our usual joke is: if I take power, he goes to the camps; but that is another story.) I also follow explicitly his thesis about the conditions of philosophy: that philosophy is by definition excessive; that it literally exists only through the excessive connection to external conditions, which are of either an amorous, political, scientific or artistic nature.

Lastly, another critique, even if a very friendly

one: our different assessments of Kant could represent a disagreement between us. And I would like to ask you, perhaps only rhetorically, if you are not also of the opinion that there is – despite the many terrible things that I too have said about a specific neo-Kantianism – something in Kant that is worth saving. What? What interests me in philosophy above all is that moment of foreignness to which you refer. Isn't foreignness at the beginning of philosophy? The so-called Ionian philosophers of nature emerged in what is now Turkish Asia with the development of commodity production. I don't want to draw here the vulgar-Marxist parallel that commodity production means abstraction and this abstraction of the commodity lies at the foundation of philosophical abstraction; where I want to steer our interest is towards this moment of foreignness that emerges through displacement; that philosophy – this is what Heidegger wants to tell us – was from the very beginning not the discourse of those who feel the certainty of being at home. It always required a minimum of breakdown of the organic society. Ever since

Socrates we always meet over and again this other-ness, these holes, and interestingly we can even discover the foreign in Descartes – and thus show up his slanderers. In the second section of the *Discourse on Method* there is, I think, his famous re-mark about how he discovered through travel not only the foreignness of other customs, but also that one's own culture is not less strange, even laugh-able, if one views it with other eyes. That is in my opinion the zero point of philosophy. Every philosopher adopts this place of displacement.

And now my question to you: I'm tempted here to rehabilitate the too often lightly taken Kantian concept of cosmopolitan civil society. This con-cept, I believe, must be brought into connection with Kant's differentiation between public and pri-vate use of reason, whose particularity consists in running contrary to intuition: what Kant names the *private use* of reason regards the work of civil ser-vants in the state apparatus. Intellectual debates, even when they are conducted in private, he calls on the other hand the *public use of reason*. What is Kant getting at? The private is for him, I believe, in the first instance the particular community rooted in a place. Kant's idea, however, is that we as intellectuals should engage in the position of the singular universal; thus, a singularity that immediately participates in universality, since it breaks through the idea of a particular order. You can be a human immediately, without first being German, French, English, etc. This legacy of Kant is more relevant today than ever. The idea of an intellectual debate that breaks through the particular order belies the conservative doctrine according to which only the complete identification with one's own roots makes it possible to be human in the emphatic sense of this word. You are completely human only when you are completely Austrian, Slovenian, French, and so forth. The fundamental message of philosophy, however, says that you can immediately participate in universality, beyond particular identifications.

Discussion

ALAIN BADIOU: First of all, I would like to say that when I have had occasion to criticize Kant, it was really a critique of what you have called 'neo-Kantianism', that is, of that sort of academic Kant which has made its return in these last ten or fifteen years as a kind of official philosophy. As far as Kant is concerned, I think it is possible to connect two of your observations. *First observation*: philosophy really needs to be able to grasp that in truths, in new problems, there is something which is irreducible to any preconceived idea of human nature. I think this is very important: there is something inhuman in what the philosopher deals with. We can give it many names. For a long time, the name for what surpasses humanity was 'God', 'the infinite', 'the intelligible', 'the absolute', and so on. We can change these names and change our conception, but I believe that in what philosophy deals with there is something that is not reducible to the human, which is to say something inhuman. Some time ago Foucault had already remarked that, after all, 'man' is a kind of theoretical construction with its own history, that we could see when man, or humanism, had begun – and Foucault added: we'll also see when it ends. That's my first remark. This is what in France was called 'theoretical anti-humanism', which was Foucault's position, but also that of Althusser and many others. When you said: 'The true problem is knowing whether there exist or not forms of radical modification of what we call "humanity"', you posed a very profound and natural question. Because 'man' designates an ideological construction, a historical construction. There is no good reason whatsoever to think that philosophy must indefinitely be used to consolidate this construction. I think that, ever since Plato, philosophy has been faced with the inhuman, and that it is there that its vocation lies. Each time that philosophy confines itself to humanity as it has been historically constituted and defined, it diminishes itself, and in the end suppresses itself. It suppresses itself because its only use becomes that of conserving, spreading and consolidating the established model of humanity. The *second observation* that one can connect, I think, to this one is when you say that in Kant we find the theme of universal singularity. You're right. More than right, perhaps. That's because in every great philosopher there is the theme of the direct participation of singularity in universality, without the detour via particularities, cultures, nationalities, gender differences and so forth. In every great philosopher there is a direct link between the singularity of thought and its universality. Today, we are constantly told that particularity is important, that the respect for particularity is fundamental. I agree with you that we should fight this reactionary refrain of cultural particularities. But we should add that the direct link between singularity and universality presupposes that there is something inhuman in universality. If we reduce universality to an ordinary human datum, this position is no longer defensible. And I believe that in Kant, this kind of direct relation between singularity and universality is linked to the moment in which Kant defines the human by means of something that exceeds humanity. The greatness of Kant is not at all to be found in his having proposed a theory of the limits of reason, a theory of the human limits of reason. This aspect of Kant exists, but today it is devoid of any genuine force. The greatness of Kant is to have combined the idea of a limit of reason with its opposite, the idea of an excess of humanity with regard to itself, which is given in particular in the infinite character of practical reason. Is man destined to finitude, including the finitude of humanity itself, of humanity as a finite humanity, or is there instead a capacity for the infinite, that is a capacity for the inhuman which is ultimately what philosophy is concerned with? That is the real question. From this point of view I will answer that yes, we can bring together your two observations, the one on the connection between universality and singularity, on the one hand, and the one on the necessity of overcoming humanism, on the other. I apologize that once again I am here in agreement with my friend Slavoj Žižek.

SLAVOJ ŽIŽEK: Unfortunately, I must also agree with you. Marx, in *Class Struggles in France*, has a very beautiful passage that explains the political dynamic of 1848: the two royalist fractions, Bourbons and Orleanists, united in the republican 'Party of Order' (*Parti de l'ordre*). Marx says that one could only be a royalist by acknowledging the anonymous kingdom of the republic. In this sense, I agree with you completely: the human as such appears only in the non-human; the non-human is the only way to be human in the universal sense in an immediate way. Why do I think that? Here I would like to come back to Kant, since I believe that Kant provides us with the conceptual instrument that allows us to think about this – by means of a seemingly secondary philosophical distinction, which, in my opinion, however, is crucial for understanding him. In the *Critique of Pure Reason*, he develops the distinction between a negative and an infinite judgement. To put it simply: the negative judgement is a judgement that denies the subject a predicate; what Kant names an infinite judgement is the kind of judgement that ascribes to the subject a negating predicate. A negative judgement exists when, for example, one says: 'The soul is not mortal.' The infinite judgement would be: 'The soul is immortal.' And what follows from that? Here, horror novels could help us, if you will allow me to call on Stephen King, my man for all seasons. We know the concept of the *undead*. What does it actually mean? Dead is dead, and if someone is not dead, they are simply alive. But when we say that someone is undead, as is said in horror literature, that is not supposed to mean that he still lives; he is dead, but not in the usual sense: he is the living dead. One sees that here another realm opens up, and my idea is that this undead is the Kantian transcendental subject. It is non-human precisely in this sense; non-human not in the sense of the animalistic, but rather, as the excessive dimension of the human itself. Seen in this way, there is something unique in that which

Kant names the dimension of the transcendental. A few days ago, a friend from Tokyo wrote to me – he knows my penchant for curiosities – that in Japan one can now buy telephones for only 85 dollars that function in a very peculiar way: you can hear the voice of the caller clearly, but there is no longer a ring tone. You merely graft a little disc onto your skull, and you receive the voice of the other vibrating directly in the eardrum. You can thus hear the other – but optimal reception arises only when you shut your ears. We are dealing here with the exception – a direct sensory perception that bypasses the sensory media. Taking a step further we can think of these remarkable experiments in brain research which are based on the idea that a feeling – for example, desire or pain – can be produced by stimulating the nerve centre directly, without going via the five senses. Why did I mention Kant here? You know the theory of schematism: in order for something really to be, it must fit certain categories. But do we not here have a type of pain that is abstract and unschematized? Not a pain of this or that, but an immediate pain? That is a little similar – please allow me this ironic parenthesis – to the first Slovenian currency in 1990–1, after independence. I loved this currency, certainly not due to pride that we had our own money, but because people did not notice that there was something a little fishy about it. After we had abolished the Yugoslav Dinar, for two years there was money in circulation with the units five, ten and so forth. No one remarked, however, that it didn't have a name: you had only 500; 500 what? Nothing more. No dollars, no schillings … Kant opened up this realm for us. And in this sense, Lacan too, in opposition to postmodernism, is correct: science is not merely a language game; it deals with the unschematized Real.

ALAIN BADIOU: It seems to me that the problem with philosophical commitment is that it is often thought to be primarily critical. Very often, one equates philosophy and critique. So that philosophical commitment would ultimately amount to saying what is evil, what is suffering, of saying what's not acceptable, or what is false. The task of philosophy would be primarily negative: to entertain doubt, the critical spirit, and so on and so forth. I think this theme must be absolutely overturned. The essence of philosophical intervention is really affirmation. Why is it affirmation? Because if you intervene with respect to a paradoxical situation, or if you intervene with regard to a relation that is not a relation, you will have to propose a new framework of thought, and you will have to affirm that it is possible to think this paradoxical situation, on condition, of course, that a certain number of parameters be abandoned, and a certain number of novelties introduced. And when all is said and done, the only proof for this is that you will propose a new way of thinking the paradox. Consequently, the determinant element of philosophical intervention is affirmative – a point on which I agree with Deleuze. When Deleuze says that philosophy is in its essence the construction of concepts, he is right to put forward this creative and affirmative dimension, and to mistrust any critical or negative reduction of

81

philosophy. When you just said that we should understand 'inhuman' as something other than a negation, I am obviously entirely in agreement with you. Once again I regret to say that we continue to be indefinitely in agreement, which besides proves that we engage in affirmation and not negation. 'Inhuman' must be understood as the affirmative conceptual element from within which one thinks the displacement of the human. And this *displacement of the human* always presupposes that one has accepted that the initial correlation is the link between the human and the inhuman, and not the perpetuation of the human as such.

Let me take an ideological example. At the end of the seventies, we witnessed the appearance, in France, of what was called '*nouvelle philosophie*' [the new philosophy]. The real creator of *nouvelle philosophie* in France was André Glucksmann, who just the day before had been a Maoist: such are the reversals of History. Glucksmann's fundamental thesis, which he continues to uphold today – that is, in his support for the USA in its war against Iraq – is that it is not possible to unify consciences around a positive vision of the Good. One can only unify consciences in the critique of Evil: this is the pivotal thesis of his entire intellectual itinerary. This negative position defines a philosophical intervention of an entirely specific sort: the philosopher is a kind of physician. He diagnoses evil, suffering, and, if need be, he suggests remedies in order to return to the normal state of affairs. For example: given that Saddam Hussein is a horrifying despot, one must employ against him vigorous therapeutic means – and these were employed, as you know, at the cost of a hundred thousand Iraqis, as of today. The American army is in the process of killing the patient, but you've got to do what you've got to do. Glucksmann is happy. He entirely subscribes to an integrally critical vision of philosophical intervention.

For my part, I think it is important to defend a wholly other conception of philosophical intervention. It is not for nothing that the first great philosophical idea was Plato's idea of the Good.

Discussion

Plato had understood perfectly well that at a given moment it is the element of inhuman affirmation which is decisive, that it is this element which carries a radical choice. If tonight you haven't exactly witnessed a confrontation, it is because with regard to this crucial point Slavoj and I are on the same side. So that there can't be a major contradiction between us.

ŽIŽEK: My paranoid reply to that would be: what if you are a liar and only pretend to think like me? The more you agree with me, the more you are in danger. Paradoxically, we share with the postmodern critical pessimists the focus on the inhuman. In the postmodern ideology of the inhuman, the inhuman is a terrifying excess that must absolutely be avoided. This ideology can even absorb a certain aspect of Lacan. There is this mythology of the terrifying – you shouldn't get too close to the fire, you have to keep the right distance; that idea that we, as in Edgar Allan Poe, live in a world on the edge of the abyss and that it is just a matter of maintaining the appropriate

84

distance: not in order to act as if there were no rad-ical evil, but merely in order to be sure that you don't fall for it. That is of course the exact oppo-site of what we propagate as the inhuman: the in-human as a space of redefinition.

Here I want to go back briefly to Richard Rorty, who I admire, as I have already said, because of his honest radicality. What is problematic is that for him the ultimate truth consists in the truth of the suffering of an individual: it should be open to each of us to give expression to our specific ex-perience of suffering. That leads us, I think, to the assumption of a false type of incommensurability. At the foundation of Rorty's conception lies a ref-erence to particularism, whose disastrousness you have already criticized in your *Ethics*. It is a ver-sion of political correctness: only a black, lesbian single mother knows about the suffering of a black, lesbian single mother and so forth. Deleuze already protested strongly against this, because he said that this type of reference always amounts – even when it appears in the short term to be emancipatory – to a reactionary position. Rorty's concept of telling stories of suffering correspondingly demands an ethics that holds the space open in which anyone can tell their story. With this we lose any serious concern with truth. The only bad thing, the model of moral negativity, would be moral violence: for example, if I dictate my concepts to others. This concept is a catastrophe. I say that even though I often find Rorty's political attitude to be congenial and even though he is often more progressive than many of the US American careerist deconstructionists. And I must add: perhaps this concept is today even the true moral catastrophe, since it prevents what you call a clear and radical choice.

Only a small improvisation: in order to confirm what you said about the negating attitude, I have to go back again to the Frankfurt school. Here we recognize where the mistake of this attitude lies. What shocks me above all about Horkheimer – for me it is Horkheimer much more than Adorno who is the actual culprit – is the glaring inconsistency of two attitudes: on the one hand, he represents the typically pessimistic perception of the dialectic of Enlightenment: all of Western history culminates in the *administered world*, the world of the completely regulated one-dimensional man, in the technological society that leaves no space for critique and so forth. Everything is manipulated – a vision of catastrophe that he unfolded in his last big publication, *Critique of Instrumental Reason*. However, whenever the same Horkheimer was confronted with a concrete political decision, he decided for the defence of this society of the ultimate catastrophe and spoke against any alternatives. In this case he was completely open. For example, he didn't want to participate in any anti-Vietnam war demonstrations and said instead: 'wherever American soldiers intervene, they bring freedom. I support that.' Adorno, here a typical opportunist, wanted just as little to take part in Vietnam war demos; it was only that he found it difficult to say this: he took refuge instead in excuses: he said once to the demonstrators that he would gladly come, but was too old and fat, and anyway the people would merely laugh if he were to come – classic Adorno.

Discussion

I wanted to draw attention to this paradox: one paints a bleak picture of the catastrophe of society and at the same time any alternative to it is supposed to be much worse. In a *Spiegel* interview that was published shortly after his death, Horkheimer speaks extensively about the administered society and continues: nevertheless – we, the developed Western society, are the island of freedom and this should be protected all around from barbarism … From this, I believe, we can deduce the sad philosophical teaching that an apparently radical condemnation of evil can perfectly take over the function of blocking any alternatives. That is a paradox of negating thought to which you just referred.

BADIOU:I simply wanted to say that there is a different way of speaking about this paradox. Today there is an entire strand of political literature which carries out a radical critique of the economic order, but which contains a no less radical support for a certain political form. This is absolutely common. Today, innumerable people are fierce anti-capitalists: capitalism is frightful, it is an economic horror, and so on. But the same people are great defenders of democracy, of democracy in the precise sense that it exists in our societies. In truth, we are dealing with the same paradox as the one you highlighted: one develops a sort of radical, objective critique of the economic form, while remaining a great supporter of representative democracy. There is a statement by Rorty that really struck me, a very important statement, which says that 'democracy is after all more important than philosophy'. While this statement may appear banal, its propaganda content is truly remarkable. Can a philosopher affirm that a political form is far more important than his own activity? I think that in fact this strange statement carries a repressive content. It is intended to prohibit philosophy from asking what the veritable essence of that which today goes under the name of 'democracy' is. I would absolutely invert the traditional approach of critique. Today's great question is not the critique of capitalism, on which more or less the whole world is in agreement with regard to the appalling material injustices, the thirty million dead in Africa because they do not receive medications, the atrocious disparities in the planet, and so on. All of this can be referred back to capitalism, in the wish for a capitalism that is better, a more moderate capitalism, and so on, without advancing an inch. Because the real question is not there, it does not lie in the negative and verbal critique of capitalism. The real question is that of an affirmative proposition regarding democracy, as something other than the consensus on the parliamentary form of politics. This is what the paradox that you point to tries to conceal, in other words, that the truly risky philosophical imperative, the one that really poses problems for thought, is the critique of the democratic form as we know it. That is the heart of the problem. And it is altogether more difficult than acknowledging along with everyone else the extent of capitalism's injustice.

ŽIŽEK: Now, I think, we are touching the really delicate theme – God, it's becoming boring – of our agreement: delicate, because I have paid dearly for the agreement in this case. Do you know how much this book on Lenin cost me?[2] I lost two-thirds of my friends because of it. You can refer to Marx without any problems: *Capital* – what a brilliant description of the capitalist dynamic, of the 'fetish-character of the commodity', of 'alienation'. But if you refer to Lenin, that is another story, a completely different story. It is unbelievable how everybody said to me afterwards that it was merely a cheap provocation. Excuse me, but when I organized a colloquium in Essen, as I later found out, the German secret service popped up and asked my secretary what we were doing. You see: it is not as tolerated as it seems. That is the paradox of today's situation: according to the official ideology, everything is allowed, there is no censorship, and everything goes off neatly. But we shouldn't be deceived. I'd like to give you an example, a mad but true example that is characteristic for our time. As I heard, in some

[2] [Translator's note: Zizek refers to *Revolution at the Gates. Zizek on Lenin: The 1917 Writings*, London: Verso, 2002.]

91

radical communities in the US – I'm using the word 'radical' here ironically, in the sense of political correctness, which in reality is pseudo-radical – the following idea is debated in all seriousness: What about the rights of necrophiliacs? Why are they cruelly forbidden to play sex games with dead bodies? The suggestion is thus: some of us consent to donating our organs to medicine in the case of an unexpected death; why not consent to having my body played with by necrophiliacs, should I die unexpectedly? Now that sounds extremely radical, but is really nothing more than a typical example of what Kierkegaard – correctly, I think – emphasized: the only true neighbour is a dead neighbour; at least in a certain ideological version of love for one's neighbours. That is what we really mean today when we treat the neighbour politically correctly. He would be better as a dead neighbour. For me that is the best metaphor for political correctness. Why? Let's ask ourselves: what does this form of tolerance really mean when it is practised in our Western societies? It means the exact opposite of what we assume. Tolerance means: no harassment. Harassment is a key word. Fundamentally, what this says is: hide your desire; don't come too close to me. It means, as I have experienced in the US: If you look too long at somebody, a woman or whoever – that is already a visual harassment; if you say something dirty – that is already verbal rape. That shows us that tolerance in this context is precisely a form of intolerance: intolerance for the closeness of the other.

However, I would like to come back once again to my real theme. As we have seen, all possible excesses seem to be allowed. Just try once, however, to touch the fetish of democracy and you will see what happens. And I agree with you: we should try to do that today, at least – to express myself briefly – for three reasons. First, we have to ask ourselves: what does democracy really mean today? How does it function? What we can least overlook is not, for example, that it is of the people and for the people, but rather that we accept determinate rules that we obey – whatever the result may be. For me Bush's election victory in 2000, if it was that, was the apex of democracy.

Why? Because no democrat at any moment even thought of not acknowledging the election result and going to the streets – even though everybody knew that they had cheated in Florida. It was clear the whole time that despite the manipulations there were rules that had to be upheld no matter what. And therefore democracy means today in the first place, even in the case of vulgar injustice, 'injustice rather than disorder', as Goethe is supposed to have said. So much for the first concrete meaning of democracy and the first reason for laying hands on it. I would see a second reason in the fact that there is an opportunism within democracy, an opportunism in the sense of a flight from the act. Here I would like to cite respectfully the German theoretician of the risk society, Ulrich Beck. He gives us to understand that the risks that confront us today are radical risks. It is not a case of breaking the influence of the great entrepreneurs, those who are responsible for environmental destruction, and of bringing in specialists in order to manage to take the correct decision; rather, it is about having to make a choice. We are all continuously confronted with a choice in which we must decide without any reason. Often the democratic representatives, however, speak only to the fetish of democracy. A way of avoiding the risk of decision is to barricade oneself behind the voters: it is not my decision, even if I legitimate it; we are all in the same boat … Our second point of critique thus aims at the fact that democracy – as process of decision – is a way of concealing decisions. That looks roughly like this: 'I am not the one who really decides; I only make suggestions. You, the people, are the ones who make the decisions.' Here one would rather follow Lacan, who said that also in the political act one must take the risk completely upon oneself. On the third reason: in *The Communist Manifesto*, Marx famously wrote that communism was accused of abolishing private property: but capitalism itself had already done that. Something similar, I think, is happening today with democracy. There is a whole series of symptomatic indications of this; for example, the renewed popularity of Ralf Dahrendorf or Leo Strauss. The usual story goes like this: democracy?

Discussion

Yes – but only for those who are also mature for democracy. Now, we all know what sort of a dead-end the US is facing in Iraq. If they introduce democracy – and with democracy I don't mean any authentic form of democracy, but rather, our beautiful, corrupt multi-party democracy – that would probably mean the electoral victory of the Shiites. And one notes all the current 'rethinking'; it is a key word: some US philosophers, Alan Dershowitz for example, are of the opinion that we should rethink human rights and change them to the extent that in certain cases torture is permissible. Here it is not just a case of the question: democracy or not. It is decisive to see what actually goes on in democracy. If there is a symbolic meaning – I hate the idea – of September 11, then in my opinion we should look for it in connection with the date 1989. For me, 1989 was not the end of utopias, as is commonly claimed, not the end of communism, but rather the unleashing of the great utopia of liberal capitalism, marked by Francis Fukuyama's 'End of History'. And September 11 is the answer to it; if it means anything at all, it means that this utopia is today dead. The Americans, I think, are paying the price in the meantime: look at American politics – it has been completely transformed. We don't have to believe their phrases about democracy any more. They want to combine their world, their power to be able to intervene militarily in the world wherever they want, with a new isolationism, new walls, etc. And democracy is defined in such a radically new way in this process that only its name remains. Something similar happens with the economy, namely, with the WTO and the IMF. Here I agree in part with a book that, in other respects, I fundamentally reject: Hardt and Negri's *Empire*. People like Lafontaine in Germany were fooling themselves if they believed that decisions could be democratized that are made on this economic level. How do you democratize the banking institutions? That is impossible already for structural reasons: should for example four and a half billion people elect the supervisory board of the IMF? We would have to conclude: economic growth and global-capitalist processes structurally exclude democracy – even in the form that capitalism itself ascribes to it.

We should consider all this if we are supposed to come to a decision for or against democracy. I'm inclined here to bring in Lukács, who said in *History and Class Consciousness* that it is a question of tactical consideration. Sometimes great things are achieved in a democratic way, for example when there is a completely unexpected result in an election. That is for me a beautiful, almost sublime moment: when we leftists support a good thing, but secretly believe however that the people are too manipulated, and yet there is ultimately a miracle and the thing goes well. My problem is, however, another one: I am prepared to advocate my views in a democratic way; but not, however, to allow others to decide democratically what my views are – here I confirm my philosophical arrogance.

QUESTION FROM THE AUDIENCE: Mr Badiou: if one follows your critique of democracy, what interest can one then have in contemporary politics?

What interested you for example in the French presidential elections?

BADIOU: What interested me in the 2002 French presidential elections was not the electoral choice, it was not the question of knowing whether one should vote for Chirac or Jospin, or what one was supposed to do in the second round. I think that this kind of question has to do with the mechanisms of opinion. What interested me in this election was the extraordinary movement that emerged after the first round, when Le Pen came before Jospin. The philosophical situation was not the election itself, it was the very animated, very violent general debate – marked by demonstrations involving hundreds of thousands – which took place after the elections. What interested the philosopher once again took the form of a paradox: an electoral situation mutated into a completely different situation, a situation of demonstrations, indignation, rage, massive protest. It was that aspect which interested me. In a general sense, philosophy is not superior to journalism when it talks about a situation which is absolutely different from what it seems to be. That is why I spoke of 'a relation which is not a relation'. In my view it is always in this paradox between being and appearing, between relation and non-relation, that philosophical intervention is situated. As for the rest, knowing what ballot one is to put into the box is a question that belongs to another register. Having said that, I can speak to you about my personal case: I haven't voted since June 1968. I am a long-term non-voter …

QUESTION FROM THE AUDIENCE: An attempt to make a little mischief: in Žižek's book *The Ticklish Subject* he took over some concepts from Badiou and used them for his own theory. Badiou, do you have the impression that this happened in an adequate way, or did Žižek misunderstand you, the way Heidegger misunderstood everybody?

BADIOU: Slavoj Žižek just said that Kant didn't understand anything about Descartes, that Hegel did not understand Kant, and finally that Heidegger didn't understand anyone ... So, if we are Descartes and Kant, surely neither of us has understood the other! Fortunately, we have spoken here of the commitments and consequences of philosophy, rather than of the organization of its concepts. So that our agreement is all the greater inasmuch as we haven't exactly entered into philosophical construction itself. When it comes to philosophical construction itself, there are certainly great differences between us, and that would be another debate. In particular, I think that there are probably differences to be found in our respective notions of the event, in our conception of the real, in the function of the imaginary, and finally on politics, not as a decision but as a process. I think that on all these points there could be important discussions. But we have dealt with the question of the present, and the question of the present is, 'What are the principal forms of philosophical commitment?' And it is true that when it comes to this very important question, as we've known for some time, we're on the same side. If the word didn't have a heavy past, I would even say: we are among party comrades.

ŽIŽEK: I would like to add a word to this. It is true that I continually engage with Badiou: in all of my books since *The Ticklish Subject* I refer to his works, every new work of his leaves a trace in mine. I'm thinking for example of the book *The Century*, which unfortunately still hasn't been published even though the manuscript has been finished for three years – a crime against humanity if we think of the significance of this book.[3] There he develops distinctions of logic, purification and subtraction, which in my opinion are achievements of great significance. And thus, in my latest book, which will appear in two or three months, without advertising myself here, I've taken a radical step that leads away from my usual position, a step that was very painful for me.[4] Up until now,

---

[3] [Translator's note: *Le siècle* was published by Éditions du Seuil in 2005; English translation: *The Century*, trans. Alberto Toscano (London: Polity, 2007).]

[4] *The Parallax View* (Cambridge, MA: The MIT Press, 2006).

I've held on to the idea that the authentic experience as such, to say it simply, is that which Lacan once called *going to the end of the analytic process*; and I told myself with doubts that this process is political, even that any political activity correlates with it. I've now abandoned that. I don't believe any more that the conclusion of psychoanalysis is, if I can say it like this, the authentic form of political engagement. That is one thing. The other is: I have taken a further very risky step for which I will probably once again pay dearly in my personal relations. I have openly and crudely attacked Jacques-Alain Miller. His latest political pronouncements are, in my view, a scandal. In his book *Le Neveu de Lacan* he takes up a position against dogmatism – we know these commonplaces: one should be flexible, subversive – and takes up a particularly fatal opposition that Julia Kristeva introduced, though in another connection: the opposition of revolts and subversion, on the one hand, and revolution, on the other. Revolts are good, they bring creative energy, they make things dynamic; revolution is bad, since it introduces a new order. That is unbelievable: in a certain way, an absolute liberal vulgarity.

With Badiou, on the other hand, I feel – as Ribbentrop said to Molotov during his trip to Moscow in 1939 – 'among comrades'.